# FUNDAMENTAL

# WISDOM
## OF AN AMOROUS GENT

## AKINBOLADE OYEGUNWA

This book is dedicated to my lovely wife and queen

# ALIIAH

# Special acknowledgements go to:

Rute and an undisclosed gent, who are the untold heroes in this volume. They single handedly inspired the subject matter.

Karen and Trevor who provided the setting- guests, dinner table, and vegan fair- which all served as the back drop to the conversation which inspired this volume.

Benjamin and Chemère, for their patronage and encouragement, which helped take this conversational theme out of the limited realm of the verbal space to the more permanent domain of the printed page. Without them the realization of this publication may have never been.

Richard, the man, who birthed the man, who birthed the book, which birthed a romantic revolution. Years ago he demonstrated the practical execution of this wisdom.

Special acknowledgement goes to Jonathan Euler, a young American gent who has dedicated his life and time to bettering the lives of others, particularly in Haiti. He is heavily involved with the non-profit organization Beehive International and beyond the cost of production and publishing the profits of this book will be directed to that organization, which provides food for orphans in Haiti and is developing a agricultural training center for the Haitian people. More information about this project may be found at: Thebeehives.org/haiti/

Special thanks to Amorous Gent Michael Wogu, co-founder and creative director for the Mbarqgo fashion brand.

# PROLOGUE:

Wisdom can be found in many places, even deep down in the heart of hearts of men best known for their physical strength and transcendent style. Muhammad Ali was quoted as having once said,

"I hated every minute of training, but I said, 'I won't quit. Suffer now and live the rest of your life as a champion.'"

Even the famed martial artist and actor Bruce Lee gave the world this nugget of truth when he said,

" Mistakes are always forgivable, if one has the courage to admit them."

Not known for his physical prowess, but rather better recognized by his fantastic hair and moustache, the contributors of this book felt it was fitting to place here one last quote by Albert Einstein who said,

"You have to learn the rules of the game. And then you have to play better than anyone else."

These statements apply to the amorous gent, for in every developing relationship there is a learning curve.  In a modern society rightly striving for equality in many spheres, it still holds true that the responsibility for developing the skills necessary to successfully navigate a romantic union falls more heavily on the shoulders of the gentleman. The process is undoubtedly challenging, but this book takes high yield essential wisdom and distills it into a potent extract, thus rendered in this quick and manageable guide to smoother and sustainable interactions between an amatory duo.

CHAPTER 1

IN RESPONSE TO GENERAL BENIGN REQUESTS FROM YOUR SPECIAL LADY, JUST SAY

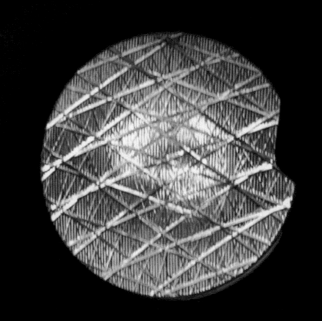

# CHAPTER 2

WHEN
SHE
IS UPSET,
JUST
SAY

12

SORRY

CHAPTER 3

WHEN
YOU
HAVE DONE
SOMETHING
REALLY
BAD,
JUST SAY A
COMBINATION OF

CHAPTER 4

LASTLY,
WHEN IT
COMES
TO
OTHER
WOMEN,
JUST SAY
20

NO

21

NO
THANKS

FUNDAMENTAL
WISDOM
OF AN
AMOROUS
GENT

F.W.A.G.

LET HER WIN. THIS TENDS TO END WELL. —FWAG

A REAL MAN SAVES
HIS AGGRESSIVE
MEAN MONSTER SIDE FOR
THE GYM...NOT
FOR HIS LADY.
-FWAG

BEFORE
YOU
DO
OR SAY SOMETHING STUPID
CONSIDER THAT
IT'S EASIER
TO NOT BREAK
SOMETHING (A HEART,
TRUST, EGG... ) THAN IT
IS TO UN-BREAK IT.
-FWAG

29

BASICALLY,
JUST
BE
EMOTIONALLY
INTELLIGENT
& LOVE
EACH OTHER

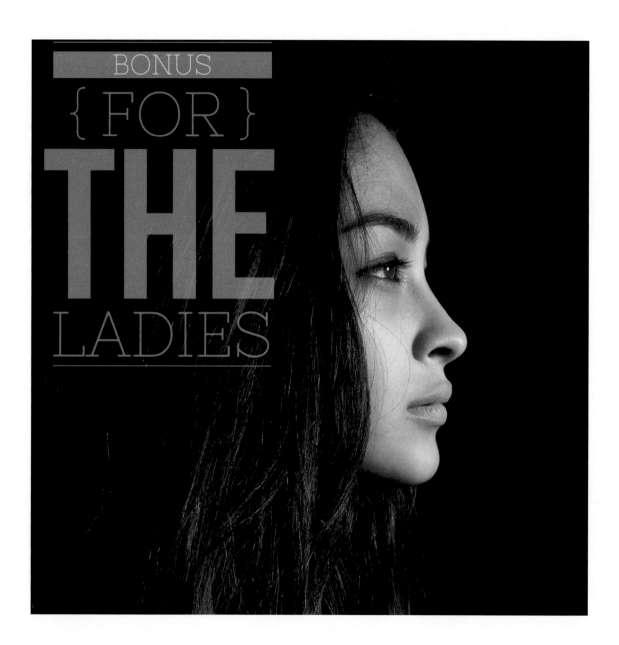

FOCUS
ON
THE
POSITIVE
{ -FWAG }

THINK BEFORE WOUNDING
**YOUR**
SOLDIER
OF LOVE
—FWAG

MAKE IT
EASIER
ON US
BY
SMILING
&
{ SAYING }
"PLEASE"
—FWAG

34

SAY "THANK YOU" OFTEN
& IN AS MANY WAYS
YOU
CAN
FWAO

## Bonus practice page:

Please insert the correct response to the following statements directed at you, the amorous gentleman.

I feel like you aren't listening to me! _____

Did you forget our anniversary again? _____

Do you think Jennifer Lopez is prettier than me? _____

Can you hold my hand and be more affectionate?_____

It seems like you prefer to watch football than go out with me? _____

Correct answers: 1. Sorry; 2. Yes and Sorry; 3. No; 4. Yes; 5. if the answer is yes definitely follow it by saying sorry

Wild card: In especially difficult circumstances, instead of answering directly you can always opt to fake a seizure (do not do this while driving, swimming, or operating heavy equipment; this tactic may not work if your partner is a board certified physician)

Prophylactic advice: She will complain less and be less likely to ask tough questions if you regularly provide positive feedback, heartfelt compliments and show your affinity for her in a way that effectually assuages her particular temperament.

Disclaimer: Please ingest the principal and understand this is just a guide and does not adequately provide all acceptable responses. Please be honest and use common sense when applying the rules denoted herein. The author cannot be held responsible for incorrect or inappropriate use of this content. The author however will gladly take credit for positive outcomes.

# APPENDIX

Amorous Gent, imagine you only have 7 instances in which you may exercise your right to argue with your lady. When she is splenetic, annoying, and ready for a disagreement, step back and ask yourself whether the issue at hand is worth forfeiting one of your 7 arguments. If it is not, just say yes and save your fight token for a more worthy battle. In doing this you will find that your discourse will be more potent when the time comes to assert your right to insist that things be done your way.